TODDLER DISCIPLINE

How to Discipline a Toddler Without Yelling

(A Parenting Guide to Raising Your Children With the Positive Discipline)

Pauline Henley

Published By Phil Dawson

Pauline Henley

All Rights Reserved

Toddler Discipline: How to Discipline a Toddler Without Yelling (A Parenting Guide to Raising Your Children With the Positive Discipline

ISBN 978-1-77485-277-4

All rights reserved. No part of this guide may be reproduced in any form without permission in writing from the publisher except in the case of brief quotations embodied in critical articles or reviews.

Legal & Disclaimer

The information contained in this book is not designed to replace or take the place of any form of medicine or professional medical advice. The information in this book has been provided for educational and entertainment purposes only.

The information contained in this book has been compiled from sources deemed reliable, and it is accurate to the best of the Author's knowledge; however, the Author cannot guarantee its accuracy and validity and cannot be held liable for any errors or omissions. Changes are periodically made to this book. You must consult your doctor or get professional medical advice before using any of the suggested remedies, techniques, or information in this book.

Upon using the information contained in this book, you agree to hold harmless the Author from and against any damages, costs, and expenses, including any legal fees potentially resulting from the application of any of the information provided by this guide. This disclaimer applies to any damages or injury caused by the use and application, whether directly or indirectly, of any advice or information presented, whether for breach of contract, tort, negligence, personal injury, criminal intent, or under any other cause of action.

You agree to accept all risks of using the information presented inside this book. You need to consult a professional medical practitioner in order to ensure you are both able and healthy enough to participate in this program.

TABLE OF CONTENTS

INTRODUCTION 1

CHAPTER 1: TIPS TO KEEP CALM WHEN YOUR CHILD IS FRUSTRATED 2

CHAPTER 2: POSITIVE DISCIPLINE 18

CHAPTER 3: WHAT TO BEWARE OF WHEN TEACHING TODDLERS 24

CHAPTER 4: BRAIN DEVELOPMENT AND WHY IT'S IMPORTANT 47

CHAPTER 5: MOST COMMON PARENTING MISTAKES PARENTS MAKE AND HOW TO CORRECT THEY 64

CHAPTER 6: METHODS TO ESTABLISH THE DISCIPLINE (RULES AND LIMITS) 75

CHAPTER 7: PROMOTING GOOD BEHAVIOUR 86

CHAPTER 8: ABC OF UNDERSTANDING TODDLER BEHAVIOR 102

CHAPTER 9: DEALING WITH TANTRUMS IGNORING THEM VS. RISING YOUR VOICE 117

CHAPTER 10: STRATEGIES TO PREVENT TODDLER TANTRUMS DURING FLIGHTS 129

CHAPTER 11: TODDLER DISCIPLINE TECHNIQUES - LANGUAGE STRATEGIES FOR STRESSED PARENTS 134

CHAPTER 12: THE ABSORBENT MIND AND CONSCIOUS MIND 158

CHAPTER 13: BRAIN DEVELOPMENT IN THE EARLY YEARS 178

CONCLUSION.. 182

Introduction

This book offers practical steps and strategies for how to effectively control your toddler with out shouting or spanking, or punishing them.

In this book, you'll discover strategies to promote good behavior from your child and also strategies for correction of bad behaviors. You don't need to resort to violence or engage in power battles to force your child to listen. All you have to do is to listen and then everything else will be arranged.

Chapter 1: Tips to Keep Calm When Your Child is Frustrated

What makes it so easy to reach sixty" from "zero when our children are making us angry? I believe that it's mainly because we let ourselves reach 60, though there are many reasons. Also, for reasons, once we hit 60, and when emotions arise, we're allowing the children to see what we'll be doing instead of the reverse.

In our daily lives, we can do a variety of things. It's because we believe the need to keep our children in control, rather than stopping for a moment to think and say "Wait I'd like to have myself in control prior to reacting." Most effective method to protect yourself from being a victim is to know the reason you're heading there and what makes you get there. In reality that, in my opinion, this is probably one of the most important actions you can take as parent.

What you are referring to is "I'm not in my control" when you are making an effort to control your child's behavior rather than your stress. Before I feel better, I require you to alter your behavior.

There's a trick that your kids will typically calm down once you're in control. Be aware that composure is infectious, so and anxiety. If we, as parents, feel anxious or stressed it has been proven that this causes anxiety in our children. I'd go as far this point to say that being emotionally reactive could be your biggest worry as parent. Take the following scenario: If you're not able to reach zero or you're not able to reach zero, you're inadvertently creating the very environment you're trying to avoid.

Let's say that you're teaching your child on the best method of riding a bike. The kid isn't understanding the concept and is getting angry and irritable and is talking in your direction. You're frustrated, angry at, angry and frustrated but he won't listen and you're feeling accountable for teaching him to figure out the most effective method to use this bicycle. You begin to feel anxious about the situation. As you're at 60, you yell at your child. The result is that your daughter or son is likely to crash of the cycle. This is because he was feels so overwhelmed by the tension surrounding him and he's unable to concentrate. Being pushed to do something was what he felt and he felt reacted to his falling short. What exactly could you do? Instead of being reactive and snappy when you're feeling like you're struggling been trying to get your child to learn to ride a bicycle. Change it up and ask yourself "How do I train myself to be calm, and how can that help for my child to reach the point where he's required to get to?" Hint yourself that you're not accountable for getting him to take the bicycle, but you're able to be adamant about getting to the ground. Then, you'll think about the best way to help him study.

This is the reason why I claim that if we aren't able to relax, we'll cause exactly what we're trying to avoid -- failure. Think of someone who is calm and serene and their presence helps to bring everyone together. The impact that it has on your child as well as your entire family when you're at peace. This will allow your child to calm him or her when she's stressed or angry, and will improve his ability to do what he needs to accomplish in the midst of tense moments. In addition, for this instant you'll no longer need to fight with youbecause you've successfully eliminated that power-fighting push by keeping him quiet when he presses your buttons.

In addition, I am aware that nobody wants to be 60, and no one likes being unsatisfied. Sometimes, they don't understand the most effective way to accomplish their goals however I think that the majority of parents' goals will be to reach a point where they are at zero. It's the truth that everyone must find the most effective method to accomplish this for themselves. (I have some ideas about the best way to go about it which I'll discuss in a second.) It's all about focusing on the importance of never to lose your valuable information, and not giving the opportunity to forget it. There's a good reason for this. If we're experiencing a crisis in front of our children are born, we're expressing "There are no adults in the house." We're telling ourselves that we're not able to manage our anxiety. I'm in need of a shift in order to feel better." So the goal is to identify what's happening is causing the anxiety and to recognize the importance of getting in control, and to control ourselves once and for all. When you try to control your child's behavior to alleviate your anxiety, the message you're saying is "I'm not in control. I'm asking you to change so that I can feel better." Therefore it is important to be aware of what's happening and be aware of how vital is to be in control and to get control of ourselves. The question you're likely to ask is "Easy for you to say. What can I do to achieve this goal? Here are some things I've learned that I've learned from working with my parents that I've found be helpful.

1. Take the responsibility to not let it go. Be aware that you're going to have to do your best to be in control from the moment from now. What's the thing that

gets you off? Is the child's attitude towards you? Do you feel like back-talk is pushing you to the limit? It's not always straightforward, and I'm sure it's not easy for anyone to control their temper for all time, but making that first commitment to yourself is the first step towards peace for all of your family members.

2. You can be sure that your child will make you feel pressured. We usually get angry when our children don't do the things we want to see them accomplish. In our minds we get stressed out our children aren't doing an adequate job. We stress that we don't know what actions to take to get our children under control. We often wonder whether this is how they'll be for the duration all their lives. We traverse a myriad of beliefs that are not right. In doing so we increase our anxiety in a negative to a great extent. The best solution is to be prepared for the child to

press your buttons, but not take it personal. In a way your child is doing his role (being an infant who isn't able to yet address his issues)--and your role is to remain calm so that you can direct your child.

3. Be aware of what you aren't accountable for. There's a lot of confusion for many parents on what we're accountable for or what's accountable for. Should you feel that you're that you're responsible for items that don't belong into your "box"such as things which are related to him getting his homework completed or showing up in time -- it could cause frustration. The items don't stay in your box , they go into your child's box. If you believe that you're the sole responsible for what happens in the end, you'll engage in actions which are likely to cause more stress and anger in your child. You could then declare, "I'm responsible

for assisting you in determining the best solution to the problem. However, I'm not accountable for fixing the problem for the benefit of you." He's probably not going to believe that he should solve the issue on his own if you consider yourself to be the one responsible for fixing your child's issues. You're not responsible for convincing your child or teen to listen to you However, you're the one who decides what you'll do to the situation when he doesn't pay attention to you.

You'll become more calm with this sort of thinking. If you're feeling accountable for having your child to think about it, how did you intend to accomplish this? How can anyone convince someone else to take action; are we supposed to dictate what others do? If your child doesn't take the initiative make a decision to be accountable for the way you want to manage your child. Consider the kind of results you'd like to award, according to what you're able and unable to accept as a reality. Your final outcome. If you want to be a leader in the future being able to stand up for yourself will enable you to be the person your children would like to be.

4. Make preparations in advance. If your anxiety is high Find out and try to prepare for it. You can observe that each morning at 5 o'clock, everyone is an anxious time. Everyone is at home from work or school hungry and exhausted. For many it's a dreadful moment of the day. Everyone's stress levels are high and the patience level is at its lowest. Take a look at, "How am I likely to deal with this situation once I am aware that my child will scream at me? What can I do if she is aware that I'm going to be silent when she insists on using the car?" Prepare yourself. Say, "This I'm not engaging in a fight with her. There is no way to force me to do this. I'm not willing

to give her permission to push me with my pants." Your position should be "No regardless of how hard you try to force me into a battle It's not going to take place." Allow yourself to be guided by the way you want to portray yourself as a parent and your current feelings.

5. Take a deep breath. Relax as you begin to feel your body swell and take a few minutes to reflect on the situation. There's a difference between reacting and responding. You're taking time to think about what message you'd like to communicate by responding. You're on autopilot whenever you react. It is important to respond to what your child is doing or saying however much you could. Be sure to breathe deeply as it gives you the chance to think about what you'd like to convey prior to reacting to your child.

6. Ask yourself "What's been able to help me before?" Begin thinking what's helped you manage your anxiety in the past. You should give yourself an instant to complete whatever it is you're required to do to feel more calm. I'm always required to get up out of the room. Sometimes, I have to take a trip to the bathroom or to the bedroom, but I only leave the issue for a short time. Keep in mind that there is nothing wrong with the way you go. There is no need to be a response to your child.

Consider it in this way: we're going to be more insistent when we're anxious and trying to convince our child to behave in the way we'd like. We're trying to manage them better, talk something that makes sense to them or make them more rounded and yell harder. Then we move to 40 instead of 20, and the number keeps increasing. It could be a sign of the day's time. Perhaps your child had an uneasy day and then we react to their mood. They react in a way which only increases. The anxiety feeds itself.

7. Consider a thought what you want your relationship to look like. What do you want to have your relationships with child to look in the future? Start thinking about what you'll need in the event that the current situation doesn't reflect how you would like your relationship to be in the next 25 years. Consider, "Is how I'm reacting towards my child helping? That doesn't mean that you should take care of your kid's requires all the time. Respecting the rules at home and delivering results in the event that your child behaves badly is an aspect of being a good loving, loving parent. What it could be referring to is take the time to deal with your child in the manner that you would like him to behave. You should ask yourself "Will my actions be worth it?" Will your reaction

bring you closer to your goal, in the event that your goal is to build a lasting relationship with your child?

8. Put some slogans on your head. Repeat them to yourself each whenever you feel your mood increasing. It could be something as simple as "Breath" and "Stop" and "Slow down" to "Does it really matter? " or " Do you think it is significant?" Whatever words will direct you to, you must take this time to go through an order of precedence. Personally, I maintain an image of my brain to help me relax and I visualize an attractive area within my head that relaxes me and frequently helps me to relax. Try to imagine the mental picture by yourself. Your ability to see it easily will increase when you start practicing this.

If your child is bothering you, the way you think in that particular moment is crucial.

The main goal is for us to remain as neutral as possible in our interactions in our lives and with our children. "What's the child up to? ask? What's he trying to do? Are they responding to the stress at home?" You don't need for the man to listen to you, but you need to understand what's happening and figure out how you're going to react to whatever's taking place.

Thinking can help us breathe and stay be calm. Being calm allows us focus on thinking that is more productive. Notes about ourselves help stimulate the thinking portion of our brain and reduces the amount that is "emotionality" that can get in the way of better thinking.

This is what we're actually talking about Responding, not just reacting. One of my teachers once said "Response is a word that comes from the phrase "your obligation." When we are able to put our thoughts before our emotions, we'll be able improve as parents. This is the goal.

Chapter 2: Positive Discipline

Discipline, as described is a type of instruction that is designed to establish a pattern of behavior that is good for children. Many parents misunderstand the concept for something that is only able to be accomplished through physical means such as "scaring" children to submit. Psychologists and parents refer to this as the "power struggle" in which parents and children fight to get the upper hand in the situation, by any method that can be used.

Discipline is a positive and not demeaning type of education that children follow the rules they are taught because of habit, not because of fear. The majority of people prefer calling it Positive Discipline to differentiate it from the kind of discipline that many are accustomed to. This is how Positive Discipline is implemented:

Easy Words as well as Tone of Voice

Toddlers don't understand every word you say at the very least, not yet. If you are disciplining your child make use of short and simple phrases to aid your toddler comprehend the meaning of your words. Keep in mind that their vocabulary may not be as wide as adult's, and they comprehend what you are saying most effectively when it isn't too precise.

The tone you use to speak is also a major factor in delivering a message your child. The way you speak can mean more than the words you use. If you can reduce the volume of your voice. Explain to your child what he should not do in a calm , but clear manner. Children are able to notice the details of your voice like the tone, the pitch and the volume. They are easily affected by these things. The way you speak can easily sway your thoughts and make you appear rude and frightening.

Eliminate Bribing

Bribing is among the most effective ways to deal with problems with a toddler who is not cooperative. Many parents have been guilty of this, by offering sweets in exchange for just a bit of peace. The issue is that the silence will only last for the time there's chocolate or other reward. This does not align with what positive discipline is supposed to accomplish.

While bribing is the opportunity to solve an issue that is temporary however, it's not the best option to employ on a regular basis since it can backfire. Consider the possibility that in the future, your child may not be able to obey your orders without receiving something in return. As he becomes an adult, he will continue to adopt this attitude and expect something back in nearly every circumstance in his life.

If he isn't given something back for being a good person or a well-behaved then he'll regress and fall into negative behaviour instead. The more expectations are not met, the more he thinks it's unfair. Therefore it will be difficult for him to continue doing the right thing. This is why a limited selection of options are the best for children.

Distraction and Redirecting

There are situations when you can help your toddler distract him and redirect his attention to something constructive. It's possible to divert their attention if you are able to interfer as early as is possible during the event. If, for instance, you are able to distract your child while he's trying to open chocolate bars You can present him with another food option without touching the food item.

If you offer a substitute by offering a different option, you're taking his focus from the chocolate as you remove it from his hands. In the same way you'll not be reacting to his screaming and make him believe it was his cries that prompted you to visit. If you are able, redirect his focus from something you can't afford to buy to something that may be more interesting to him. If, for instance, your child is beginning to feel frustrated because they can't bring home an item from the store then redirect his focus by pointing out the cars that pass by outside. You could also keep him distracted by explaining what you will do when you return at home, or by providing him with a few options.

Absolutely, do not promise or bribe to give him some reward (like chocolates or Ice cream) to help calm him down. Your child can easily connect reward with anger and will soon get used to receiving treats when they are unhappy.

Chapter 3: What to Beware of When Teaching Toddlers

Many parents can attest to the fact that raising a toddler the equivalent of fighting on a daily basis. Little bundles of fun are often highly stubborn children that test the of their parents and the adults who are around them.

It's also the time of childhood in which they start with asserting their autonomy. One of the first words they speak will be "No," affirming the toddlers' desire to not be independent and do things their way. They love to run around to escape. Normal toddlers are bursting with energy. They jump, run around, play, and explore everything that interests them. They are awestruck by the sense of touchand enjoy playing with things using their senses.

Since toddlers are easily enticed by the things they see or hear and their impulsive nature could make them awkward and may cause them to be a bit numb. Parents should educate their children on safe ways to handle or touch objects and avoid touching hot objects.

While raising a toddler is lots of work watching your child grow and develops their skills is amazing. Due to the rapid changes in development that take place during the toddler years it is essential to employ a disciplined approach which will help the child gain independence, while also teaching him about how to behave socially and also other desirable qualities.

There is the assumption that parenting methods are applicable to everyone, and that children react in the same manner. Every child has their unique set of characteristics. They are part of the DNA of his parents, which is inherited from parents. Some toddlers are quiet or even-tempered, whereas others are outgoing and possess the characteristics of aggressive children.

If you can understand your child's unique character and normal behavior, you can assist him adapt to the world. It is important to be able to work with the child's personality, not against it, while taking into consideration the following elements you should take into consideration when disciplining your child. Making sure that your child is properly cared for and fed by providing healthy and positive activities while instilling positive and discipline are crucial for his mental, physical emotional, social and behavior development..

It is a. Behaviour and Temperament

Temperament is the genetically based and heritable element that affects the way of conduct and behavior of an individual. The traits that a child exhibits in his early years generally predict the temperament of his adult.

The behavior of a child is the result of his temperament as well as the progression of his mental, emotional and physical development. The way he behaves is determined by the beliefs he holds regarding himself, you and the world as a whole. Although it is innate and natural but there are ways to assist your child in managing it in a positive way.

The nine dimensions of or the traits that are related to temperament

The activity level refers to how much physical activity your child exhibits during certain activities. This also includes his non-active period.

Are your children unrestful and unable to stay still for longer or is always looking to move about?

Are you a parent to a child who is quiet and loves to play by himself or watching television?

The term "rhythmicity" is used to describe the predictability or uncertainty of biological and physical functions, such as eating, bowel movements and sleep.

* Do your children thrive in routines and follows regular sleeping or eating patterns?

* Does he exhibit an unpredictable personality and is he averse to routine?

Persistence and attention span are the abilities needed to stay in the present for some time.

* Does your toddler stay to an activity?

* Does he get easily annoyed and is he looking for something else to do?

The Initial Reaction (Approach or Refusal) is the term used to describe the reaction to something unfamiliar and new. It is the initial reaction towards a stimulus such as the new person, place or toy, as well as food. His response is reflected in the mood of his face, facial expressions such as smiling or motor activities for example, like reaching for an object or gulping food. Negative reactions can are crying, withdrawal and wailing or even spitting out the food.

* Is he cautious or wary of situations or people?

* Does he enjoy new faces and is he able to cope with the new settings?

The degree of response is correlated with the degree of reaction to any particular event or circumstance. Toddlers react differently to the things happening surrounding them. Some shout with joy or smile with joy, while some make noises, and some are unable to react to what's taking place.

Do you find yourself constantly trying to figure out how your child will react when they are upset about something?

Does your child display his emotions?

Adaptability refers to the ability of a child to adapt to changes as time passes.

* Does your child have the capability of adjusting to sudden shifts in plans or interruptions to his routine?

* Do you think he has difficulty to adapt to changes and resist them as hard as the best he can?

Distractibility is the child's ability to become distracted. It is a result of the impact of an external stimulus on the child's behavior.

* Can your child concentrate on his task despite all the distractions around him?

* Does he find it difficult to focus when there are people or other activities in the surrounding?

The mood of your child is directly determined by how your child views the world through his own eyes and with a clear understanding. Some respond with joy and acceptance, and others frown in displeasure "because" it feels it.

* Does he show mood fluctuations on a regular basis?

Does he usually seem to be happy?

Sensory Threshold is connected with sensitivity to sensory stimulation. The children who have sensitivity to stimulation require the gradual and careful introduction to new individuals as well as experiences, objects, or experiences.

Are your children attracted to flashing lights, loud noises or the texture of food?

* Does he not seem to be bothered by such things and accepts them for what they are?

There are three kinds of toddlers:

* Feisty or active toddlersThe children of this group possess a lot of energy. They exhibit even in the infancy of their mothers' uterus including lots of moving and kicks. When they are infants they play in a squirming, crawling, and bouncing around the entire places. As toddlers are active, they run, climb around, jump, and

play a lot of fidgeting to let their energy flow. They are excited when they do things, or are anxious about strangers or situations that are new to them.

They are naturally enthusiastic they are joyful and happy and love the joy of having fun. However, if they're unhappy, they'll be loud and clear about it. They are also demanding and difficult to incorporate into regular routines.

Help him achieve:

Be aware of his personality and be aware of his triggers.

Help him learn self-help strategies to keep going when his energy levels are low, or to calm himself when his level of activity is extremely high. A few simple and effective methods to help calm yourself are to count between 1 and 10 and taking deep breaths, performing jumping jacks to rid yourself of energy and then redirecting him to different activities.

Create a routine for the day which includes play, as well as other activities that help to improve the gross motor skills of your child. Offer him the chance to play safely and to explore. It is important to ensure that your child is safe in your home.

Make sure that he gets a nap. A relaxing afternoon nap can rejuvenate the body and mind of your pet which will help prevent temper tantrums and mood swings.

Don't let him spend time in front of an electronic device or perform things that are not interesting. Make him feel more active by taking him out to have fun in the open air.

Become a calming influence. Know how your temperament influences your child's temperament, and discover ways to be an example.

* Cautious or passive toddlers- They like activities that don't require much physical exertion, are slower to move and prefer to sit in a more regular manner. They're slow to warm up when meeting strangers and tend to withdraw when they are confronted with an unfamiliar environment. They require a lot of time to finish their work.

Help him achieve:

If your child isn't as active, establish goals or deadlines that make him finish the tasks assigned to him.

Invite him to engage in a game with fun sounds and bright toys or gentle persuasive techniques.

Always emphasize the positive. Give them praise and encouraging words when you see your child's efforts being displayed or when they reach easy milestones.

* Flexible or easy toddlers These kids are flexible, usually peaceful, and content. Sometimes, however, they are easily distracted and require lots of encouragement and affection from you.

Help him achieve:

Be realistic and anticipate mood fluctuations when something is not flowing smoothly. Don't get too harsh on your child when the child displays an unusual outburst.

Give him activities that are interactive and invite him to join you. Sometimes, it's easy to let him play on his personal devices due to his jovial nature. It is important to offer different options to help him improve the skills of his.

Look for the warning signs and figure out the reason for small changes to attitude and behavior towards things. Keep an eye out and plan an exclusive moment for him.

B. Nine Strategies for Toddler Discipline

Discipline is a problem for many parents, particularly those with young children. They are looking for the most effective method to raise well-mannered and confident children that are capable of handling the demands of life.

In terms of technicality, there is no correct or incorrect method, except for the punitive methods which can scar children for the rest of their lives. The only thing you need to do is determine the appropriate disciplinary approach that is compatible with your child's unique temperament, personality and temperament.

Here are some easy methods widely used by parents across the globe:

Recognition and Encouragement

The words of praise and encouragement always yield positive results encouraging toddlers to exhibit good behaviour. Offering your child small rewards or applause after he has done something admirable will motivate him to keep improving his abilities. Appreciating good behavior will encourage him to do the same action again and repeatedly to earn your praise and approval.

Rethinking

Change the tone and content of your conversation or rethinking your ideas often will result in positive reactions.

Instead of giving a directive which uses "don't do this" or "get this" reconsider your approach to reflect a request. It's better to make use of phrases like "would you...if it's fine to you?"

Be aware that your child isn't your mini-you. It is also helpful to look at things from his point of view. For example, if the child doesn't want to be in the child's car seat. You could think "I realize that you really enjoy being in your automobile seat. However, it's similar to this seat belt that I use. They keep us safer." By doing this way you're teaching your child the importance of safety by using the appropriate tools.

Disregard

The act of not ignoring tantrums or fits deliberately conveys for your child to know that you're not influenced by his behaviour and that you are not a slave to his desires. In order to make it more efficient, adults around your family must be aware of this method to discipline and end the child's behavior. This may sound cruel, but avoiding from engaging in or reacting to your child's outburst is one of the most effective ways to stop the behavior.

Not looking or ignoring the other approach is a great way to stop a child's tendency to do things that are naughty to gain your attention. Beware of looking at him or glaring at him or getting angry, as this indicates you are paying focus is on him isn't paying. It is important to behave as if you're not irritated by his behaviour and make him understand that screaming and throwing temper tantrums won't allow you to give in to his needs.

Break

It's also known as an "in-time-out," a well-known method used by parents to enforce discipline on their children. The concept is to take him to a particular "cozy area" within your home, a certain area which is secure and free of distractions or distraction. Then, let him think about the behavior he has displayed. It is essential that you are able to observe him and be sure of the safety of him. When you have reached a certain point in the break, you should discuss the incident, and give him the opportunity to clarify and admit the error.

A best general rule for setting the duration of a break must be proportional to the age range of your child. For instance, when your child is 2 years old, you should give him the 2-minute timer. But, you should use this technique carefully and don't make the child feel alone or lonely.

Substitute and Distraction

If your child is prone to this habit of hitting objects in the home, such as banging his toy across the table, try to distract him from doing it again. It is possible to draw the attention of your child by providing him with something. Children are easy to distract since they typically have a limited attention span. You could also replace his toys, reorienting him to something that's more interesting.

Toddlers aren't aware of the reason for being punished. Keep his attention elsewhere with an plaything or toy to draw his attention. The sound of his name grabbing his attention. Once his eyes are fixed on you, present him with something that will prompt him to join you.

Offer Choices

Allowing your child to participate in making simple decisions such as the color of shirt he'd like to wear provides him with confidence and control. It increases his self-confidence and reduces the likelihood of power battles. By engaging your son in this process you can ease the transition and make him feel proud of having made a decision.

The three methods mentioned above must be avoided as much as is possible.

Slamming into violent rage

Your child is going to be stubborn and make outbursts of anger to get you to give in to his demands. If you don't give in at first, it is an opportunity for the child to try a second trial. It's the toddler's dominance strategy . It can be avoided by not granting his demands that are unreasonable and could harm his health and safety.

Raising your voice. What is the right time to do it?

Parents have admitted that at someday or the other they shout towards their kids. Research has proven that shouting is one of the techniques for disciplining children that can cause behavior problems worse, which can weaken the bond between parent and child. Also, it loses effectiveness as time passes and your child starts to lose interest in you whenever you do it repeatedly.

Why is screaming necessary? Speaking out your feelings in public can be beneficial for both your child and you and help him to become more compassionate and recognize that he's upset. Be aware of your words. In lieu using "you" assertions, make use of "I" statements such as "I am sad because you can't play together with him" instead of "You aren't doing your best!"

It is also essential that you are aware of own mood and your behavior. Sometimes, you shout when you're unhappy or exhausted, but is not when your child did some awful thing.

Punishment

All forms of punishment that includes spanking, caning or beating, is not a good idea. It was a common practice for a while, and was used by parents to regulate their children, but numerous studies found that it led to lasting disdain and resentment. The act of smacking, for example, even occasionally, could lead to the development of anxiety in children and can make your child believe that it's fine to hit.

Children are taught to be scared of consequences if they are they are caught, yet they continue to do it even when you are not around. If you tell them, "Don't make me catch you again doing this or you'll be punished!", he may consider the action to be unintentional and must be cautious to make sure you don't find him guilty of it. This doesn't solve the issue of behavior and is unhelpful for helping the child make better choices or develop self-control. It is also a common result from various surveys that punishing children leads them to engage engaging in avoidance and rebellious.

Chapter 4: Brain Development And Why It's Important

Your child's growth rate is rapid between the ages of 1 and 4 years old however, not only in weight and height. In the realm of toddler behavior, it's essential to develop a fundamental understanding of how your toddler's personality and brain are developing. Through the years of toddlerhood, your child will make significant progress in both those areas.

The development of your child's brain plays directly in the types of behavior you could expect to observe in your toddler. They can also influence how you respond to nonproductive behavior over time, and also how you can help your child develop the skills and self-regulation required to develop into happy, healthy, and functioning individuals.

Child development is a fascinating and rapidly growing field of study. A thorough examination of all of the amazing aspects of cerebral development. But a fundamental understanding of what's happening in the mind of your child at various ages can help you make the right choices about how you engage with and support your child's increasing confidence in their own abilities.

Knowing the signs to look for and why certain behaviors occur can help you reduce your own anger when your child behaves badly.'

We'll discuss the most significant developmental milestones in relation to toddler behavior from between 1-4. Don't fret that your child hasn't checked off all the items in each category. Every child grows at their own pace and could achieve certain milestones more quickly or slower than the average toddler. If you're worried or your child appears to be lagging behind other kids be sure to consult with an experienced pediatrician to ensure that everything is in order.

12-18 months: During this stage, your child will begin using the word 'no and also make demands and follow one-step directions. There isn't much or no experience in the realm of emotional or impulse control. self-regulation. With the newfound freedom she'll soon be able to explore the surroundings independently, but she'll always need the security of her mother's presence. When she begins the process of asserting herself through speaking up as well as engaging in self-reliant physical activities, gentle discipline methods will allow her to remain in good health and safety.

This table summarizes important stages in the brain and emotional development:

Brain Development and Social/Emotional Development between 12-18 months

Expresses "no"

- Expresses desire (i.e. by the use of pointing)

• Recognizes concrete items like blankets, bottles and even books

- May follow one-step verbal commands like 'sit down or come here. The child may begin to exhibit temper anger

- May begins to exhibit an aversion to strangers

Shows love for others

- Mother may cling to her in unfamiliar situations or in situations that aren't familiar.

Use points to share fascinating discoveries with other users.

Begin exploring by going out on their own generally, so when a parentor parent is present

18 Months to 2 Years The baby in your life is well into the toddlerhood stage. In the past, he has beginning to speak in short sentences, demonstrate an increase in curiosity in other children, participate in simple games of imagination, and follows more complicated instructions. He is also able to recognize names of objects and pictures of objects and can point to them when asked. At this point the child is able to feel the full range of emotions. Due to his growing independence, his more developed emotions, and the lack of emotional control or impulse control, tantrums and refusing will start to happen. The discipline strategies you employ will

be focussed on keeping your child safe and healthy while helping them develop control over themselves. Take a look at the following table for an in-depth analysis.

Brain Development, Social/Emotional Development, by 2 years

Points to objects or images when they are referred to by their names

Able to create small phrases (2-4 words)

- Starts recognize basic colors and shapes

Begins to play basic pretend games

Follow instructions in two steps

Simulates the words and behaviors of other people

- Excited when she is in the presence of other children

Increases in independence

- Shows defiant behavior

The majority of the time they play with other children instead of alongside them, however is starting to include others in simple games like chase

3-4 years: By the time you reach your toddler has shown increasing complex cognitive abilities that include following more complex instructions as well as completing simple games. He's also capable of holding short conversations using full sentences, and displays a love of and compassion for other people. He's become more independent socially and is able to separate from his parents more easily. The terrifying twos have come in fully forcefully and you should expect more resistance from your toddler when he is exhausted or does not achieve what they want. Similar to every stage of toddlerhood, your child's discipline will always be centered on safety and health but you are now able to introduce more concrete skills like sharing, turning and better emotional control.

Brain Development Social and Emotional Development before 3 years

Follow instructions in three steps

- Have the ability to hold a brief conversation in up to 3 sentences

You can play with more complex toys that have moving parts

Plays imaginatively with other people and toys

- Are able to complete extremely simple puzzles

Replicates the behavior of other people

Shows respect for others

- Participates in turn-taking in games and other activities

Shows the concern for family members or friends who are who are in need.

- Can recognize possession ('mine" vs. "his" or hers)

- Displays a variety of emotions

- Able to roam freely without the presence of a caregiver at least a small portion of the time

It is possible to feel upset or uncomfortable by changes to routine

3-4 years: The abilities that first appeared between the ages of 12 between 12 and 36 months are continuing to grow as your toddler grows up to be able to take part in more intricate cognitive tasks like remembering nursery rhymes and starting to think about things such as timing and the contrast. They may also display an incredible amount of creativity while she engages in playful playing with herself, her toys and with others. At this point, she's likely developed a sense of self-control in regards to emotional regulation, and is experiencing fewer or shorter anger outbursts. She's made progress in controlling her impulses, but it's still an ongoing process. She's also learned to adhere to basic behavior expectations including not throwing foodat her, being non-aggressive, as well as washing up toys. In this stage of development, discipline will be more concentrated on helping your child to develop the fundamentals of essential life skills, such as co-operation and the ability to resolve conflicts.

Age Brain Development, Social/Emotional Development at 4 years old

-- Abel to sing simple poems and songs from memories

- Abel to relate stories and make predictions in the form of stories

- Knows the concept behind counting and might be capable of counting

- Begins to comprehend the notion of time

- Recognizes the notion of'same' and "different is becoming more imaginative through imaginative play

- Likes being with others children more than by herself

- Has the ability to work with other children

It's not always easy to distinguish between real and what's just a figment of imagination

Talks about interests and likes. the interests of

You can clearly see that toddler years are an important stage for the development of social and cognitive. As your child progresses through the various stages of toddlerhood There are some crucial supportive and danger factors to be aware of in your mind to ensure that your toddler's maximum cognitive and social development.

The factors that support your child's development are the environment as well as interpersonal influences that contribute to and/or promote healthy development. Risk factors however could have a detrimental adverse, damaging, or harmful impact on your child's brain and emotional/social development.

The table below provides a list of the protective and risk aspects to watch out for. It is recommended to encourage supportive factors in the home and risk factors should be minimized or eliminated.

Supportive Factors Risk Factors

- Reactive interaction with caregivers (caregiver is able to interpret and reacts appropriately to children's emotional needs in a timely and precise way)

- Love interactions

Hugs

- Adequate nutrition

- Sleeping well

- Time for secure exploration with a caregiver's presence

- Routine and structure

A lack of loving interaction from the mother or primary caregiver

- Unresponsive or invasive parenting

- Too much screen time'

- Poor nutrition

- Poor sleep

- Stress at home

Child abuse

- Child abuse during the presence of the toddler

Communication is the key to every relationship and the one you share with your child is not any different. The time from the age of one through 4 is crucial for your toddler's development of social and language abilities. Communication between your child and parents during this period of development is about effective interactions, modeling behaviours that are communicative and helping to build confidence as well as self-confidence.

One of the most important things to remember when communicating with your child is that it's an ongoing, two-way conversation. One child reaches out and while the second responds. While you and your child become more efficient and responsive ways, your child will gain an increased sense of security and confidence, as well as empathy and self-determination.

Effective Communication Effective Communication

The way parents speak communicates more than words. When you talk to your child, you are showing them how to conduct a conversation that includes important abilities like listening and empathy as well as turn-taking. When toddlers watch you talk to them and other people and learn more about human interaction will contribute to their knowledge of what it means to be able to communicate effectively and function within a social environment.

Setting a good example isn't all you have to think about. How parents communicate to their toddlers can affect how effective their communication (does the toddler grasp the message the message in a way that's feasible?) and also the toddler's development of social and emotional understanding.

Talking with your child in ways that are active or passive could result in negative effects on their social and emotional development and can hinder the advantages of teaching moments as well as healthy behavior. Instead, parents should use a firm, but respectful tone when they attempt to engage their toddlers.

With these essential factors with in our minds, lets think about some essential tips for speaking in a way that your toddler can comprehend.

Chapter 5: Most Common Parenting Mistakes Parents Make and How to Correct They

The task of disciplining your toddlers on their own is not an isolated event. Beware of the common mistakes that parents make. A lot of the mistakes made by parents can not only reduce how effective the rules you enforce on your child but can also encourage your children to behave badly. Here are some typical mistakes that parent make while disciplining their child.

Being Aggressive

Many parents quit and turn violent. The issue when you are in a state of aggression is that your children do not learn anything other than fear. They don't comprehend the importance that you would like them to understand. Instead, they obey because they fear. Research has also shown that children who have had violent parents are more likely to become more aggressive, too. Being aggressive doesn't just involve smacking your children as well as making use of offensive words or threats. It is crucial to remember that you're dealing with a toddler , and acting aggressively is not the best option you could do.

Comparisons with other parents

Stop comparing yourself to other parents. The way they discipline their kids is their own problem. If a friend of yours says that slapping your child in the face can be efficient, even if they could demonstrate it, don't take the advice immediately. According to numerous studies, hitting or slapping your children isn't the most effective method of discipline for your children.

Comparison of your child with other Children

It's not a good idea to compare your child's achievements with other children, unless it is something that makes him feel proud of himself. Do you want your child to judge yourself in terms of wealth with a parent more wealthy than you are? Absolutely you wouldn't. Similar to that it is not a good idea to be comparing your child to other children. Your child is unique in the way he is and you ought to respect him for what he has to offer.

False

Parents may lie to their children in order to get them to comply. While this might be effective from time to time however, it also comes with negative consequences. In the case study of mother from New Jersey with a 2-year-old daughter, it transpired that on a particular day, when her daughter was not keen to go out of the car. She pointed out the house of her neighbor nearby and informed her child the house was actually a child care facility filled with troglodytes from an eerie TV show. She informed her daughter she had two options: either take her car to the airport or stay in the house , with the risk to be assaulted by terrifying cavemen. Of course, she eventually caved in and walked into the car. If you examine what transpired it would appear that the event was successful. There was no shouting , spanking or other incident which took place. The issue began following the incident. In the aftermath of the case study the daughter of the mother started to be afraid of daycare facilities, believing that these places are inhabited by scary cavemen. It is evident that while the mom was able convince her child to go into cars, her result was far worse. Instead to lying the only method is to be honest and clear.

Yelling

There is no need to shout at your child just to convey your message. As per the Dr. Alan Greene, a pediatric doctor and a an instructor of medical faculty at the Stanford University School of Medicine If you lose control and begin yelling at your child, he will be prone to doing the same. However, this doesn't necessarily mean that your child is deliberately disrespecting you. This is simply a sign the fact that they are having a tough time with you as you are unable to communicate with one another. This is why you should remain quiet, but solid. Eye contact is also helpful.

Think You Know Your Toddler

In reality, it is difficult to comprehend your child. It is because toddlers don't think like adults do. It's impossible to know the extent to which certain events affect your child's thoughts and feelings. In addition, you do not know exactly to what extent. So, don't over-stress your child.

You are raising your child, and You Want

Do not force your lifestyle or your way of life on your child. Your child is the sole owner of his life. Let him go after whatever he wishes. Let him draw his goals and be confident in these dreams. Concentrate on the child you already have rather than the image of the child which you'd like to be. Your child might not be wired in the way you prefer him to be and this is perfectly normal. Let your child get his opportunity in the world. Believe in him and follow the life he wants to live.

All of it is being corrected at the same Time

Many parents attempt to address all inappropriate behaviours of their child and expect their toddler to to complete the task in the shortest time. This is an extremely unreasonable expectation. Even if you can alter your bad manners or behaviours in a short time, don't expect your child to be able to accomplish things more quickly than you do. In addition, the majority of parents are complaining about their children. are typical behaviors (or infractions) for a toddler.

It is important to learn to recognize your battles, and not try to do everything simultaneously. You can begin with the behaviour you think is one of the worst and needs focus. After you have corrected the issue then you can proceed to the next. It is important to be sure to discipline your child at every opportunity. But, it is important to learn to focus on specific behaviors, to be able to assess the efficacy of the strategy or methods you employ.

Long Explanations

Long explanations don't work with toddlers. It will appear as if you are talking in gibberish after just a few minutes. Remember they have very short attention span. Therefore, lengthy explanations will not go over well with toddlers. For instance it is not necessary to explain to your child why eating desserts before the bedtime isn't good for the teeth of her. She will be able to understand when the time comes. Instead, simply tell her, "No cookies." It is not necessary to explain it all. In the end toddlers aren't meant to be extremely logical. They don't care as for explanations. Naturally, the can be tempered by certain exceptions, for instance, when a toddler would like to know the reasoning for something or when providing an explanation seems to be the most effective way to proceed.

Bribe

Don't bribe your child just to get him to follow your wishes. In the event that he does, he'll beg for the item, and this can cause problems in the future. In a case study , mother in Montclair, New Jersey, she gave her child a small piece chocolate in exchange for the fact that the child (her toddler) was willing to eat her food. It worked. Her daughter ate her dinner quickly. At this point, it could seem that bribing could be efficient. However, what actually happened was that following the dinner she would constantly insist on her mother giving her a chocolate bar to complete her dinner.

Instead of rewarding your kid, the recommended method is to make her understand how important food is. Based on the scenario that was discussed in an in the previous study, the best approach is to tell your child that she'll become hungry later at night if she consumes a small amount of food and she won't be healthy, and this could cause her to become sick. If you are experiencing the same issue for your child explain advantages of this food, for instance, it may enhance her appearance and make her taller or more intelligent, and so on -however, do not be a liar.

Don't Ask Questions

Toddlers are usually awash with questions. As as a parent, you will want to respond whenever you can. It is important to remember that you shouldn't tell your child a lie when you ask questions. But, you are able to give funny answers, but you must be certain that your child knows you are making an act of comedy when you do it. Be careful not to give creepy answers or ones that cause fear in your child. Therefore, you should avoid answering questions which are related to ghosts or other terrifying things. But, parents are so focused on answering all the questions their children ask that they forget another crucial step to take: ask questions to their children.

If you are willing to spend the time to inquire about your child's questions, even if they are crazy and absurd ones, you could be amazed by the answers you get. Toddlers are gifted with imagination and are extremely interested and open to nearly all things. When you ask inquiries to the children you'll also learn about his thinking process, and you will be able to see how young he really is and every reason you shouldn't be abrasive or harsh with your child.

Chapter 6: Methods to establish the Discipline (Rules and Limits)

Strategies provide a framework, guidelines that indicate what behaviors are acceptable and which isn't, and should be specific, clear and clearly defined. When making boundaries, it's essential to keep the same rules in place, so that children will understand that boundaries can't be reached at different times or locations. It is important for the child to understand what boundaries establish for them aren't something that can be disputed or ambiguous. The boundaries need to be defined within a certain framework. Within that frame, rules need to be formulated. But that does not mean that these rules have to be excessively restrictive.

It is obvious that living within set limits is the most effective method for children to develop life skills and be able how to handle everyday difficulties Therefore, those limits have to be established quickly. It is also crucial to create an environment of acceptance and love prior to, not when problems occur. Boundaries, then, are the rules that define what behavior is acceptable and which not. They should be clear, precise and clearly established.

The difference between child's needs and wants

If a child asks their parents for permission to take a step parents must decide on the best answer according to the principles and values they and their family adhere to. If we are to decide to say no to anything, we must be aware of our choices in order to ensure that we don't continually alter the rules, however, at the same it is essential to remember that boundaries aren't "set in bricks and mortar," but that with time , they must be adjusted and changed in accordance with the developmental stage of the child.

When it comes to establishing boundaries, it is important to know how to differentiate between children's wants and requirements. Children often do not know their requirements, yet they know exactly what they would like. If parents only satisfy their children's desires, then children are the ones to decide what is right for them in a situation for which they're not prepared. We must be aware of the right time to tell "no," but not necessarily depriving the child of his basic desires for food clothing and footwear, health, sleep and love as well as social interactions.

The second thing to consider is to be consistent. If you're conscientious, your child will be aware that the boundaries are not able to be reached at different times or locations. It doesn't mean, however, that you have to be rigid. Sometimes, it's also important for you to be more flexible particularly when your child is able to present an argument that is convincing - to show them that we are able to respect their opinions.

A rebellion against the law

When we do not say yes kids may be upset and angry, sad or depressed and start crying. It is normal for children to express their feelings of anger and is an essential aspect of growing older. If children are upset and discontent, we must not ridicule them, emulate them, or blame their behavior, blame them (from the second year to the age of five in a kid's existence and blame directly affects the child's sense of self-worth and self-esteem) or criticize, bribe or convince them to feel guilty , or to stop talking about their emotions or to change their mind. It is essential to acknowledge the child's feelings, be able to understand them, assist them in directing their emotions, and be consistent.

It is crucial not to let your child down when he or she is crying, begging or yelling at any time demonstrating against the rules you have establish. If we allow ourselves to be manipulated then the child will begin to engage in that type of behaviour when they are in the mood for something, and then the next time, they'll resort to the same behavior repeatedly. If they learn from their families that things will happen exactly as they wish whenever they scream, cry or throw themselves to the ground, then they'll adopt similar behaviors in the kindergarten years and this makes it harder for children to interact with others.

When setting the boundaries it is essential to ensure that your child is heard and is understood It is recommended to sit with them to gaze them in the eye and express your wishes in a simple and straightforward manner that is easily understood by them. It is not a good idea to make promises or promise that you are unable to do. Don't be discouraged by the pressure of your child ("Please please, but only this time") !"), since it's normal for this will show the child that you did not think out what you were saying. If you're trying flexibility, you should do it prior to letting your child ask for something.

The most wonderful thing in the world is an embrace!

Researchers have once set out to gather evidence that shows that the affection of parents is beneficial to the well-being of children in their formative years. However, in their studies, they discovered that hugs and kisses from dad and mom mean more than they believed. Researchers believe that greater self-confidence as well as more effective communication between parents and children as well as less behavioral and psychological problems are due to the affection and warmth between the parents and their child. This is among the most essential elements of a loving relationship between parents and children that is tenderness and warmth, understanding and trust.

Do you feel that your anxiety and fatigue disappear after an exhausting day at work you get home, embrace and kiss your kids? Children also experience affection and love. However research has shown that neglecting children, which can lead to a decrease in affection and attachment, may influence the child's physical as well as mental well-being for long-term, with negative outcomes, such as low health. Children regardless of their background must be loved by their parents. The children "absorb" their meaning behind the things their parents and mothers try to accomplish for them.

Can you overdo love? Yes, sure you can. But there's a solution: be moderate.

When it comes to raising children the importance of setting personal boundaries is as crucial as love, understanding and support. When limits are set and children are taught that they're responsible for what happens to them. This aids them in self-regulation of their emotions and behavior and helps them feel secure, but also to develop a sense of confidence and security with their family members. These are vital abilities that allow children to be more successful in school and to build relationships with classmates and develop friendships. Numerous studies have shown that a learning style which acceptance, support of warmth and affection are demonstrated, and where there is a consistent and clear set of boundaries and the structure is in place, and the expectations of children are very high allows children to develop into confident secure, steady, and successful individuals who build strong relationships with other people.

There are differences between orders, boundaries, and rules

Limits can help you avoid conflict between parent and child, whereas commands are based on punishments as well as negative consequences. The boundaries you establish are not based on a child's fear of their parent and the fear of punishment and anger. They let children have positive and negative consequences in a secure and safe and loving environment with unconditional parental love. Furthermore, they let children be accountable for their own behaviour.

Children should not be threatened or blackmailed. It is preferential to give them praise and certain privileges for acceptable and desirable behaviour. If a child is acting inappropriately and in a manner that isn't appropriate It is crucial to ensure that the child is aware of the reason why this behavior was unacceptable before a particular privilege is removed. Removing a privilege must not mean removing the love of parents or limiting the fulfillment of the child's emotional and developmental requirements.

Children require guidance and direction to be able to embrace the values of their families and parents are the ones that can make this happen. Parents are the barrier between the child and wrong values that come at them from all angles Parents assume the responsibility for their child by establishing clearly, definite boundaries that they adhere to. You can't play a game if do not know the rules. Boundaries work best when they are enacted in a setting of acceptance, love, and respect.

Chapter 7: Promoting Good Behaviour

How To Create Healthy Habits

Sometimes, you don't want to be able to make your child stop their behavior with one click, before they start becoming out of control? I admit that I'd like for my toddler to have batteries that can be removed!

However, let's not forget about the switch to turn off and the battery that is removable... We must get back to the present, and we'll be content for an easy and needed stop: a brief period for us to rekindle our creativity and figure out the best method to confront the situation without worrying that our heads exploding. Because none of these ideas are even remotely likely of being realized, I'd like to suggest a way to keep from screaming at the child even when we're getting a little crazy:

If you're not upset right now, this is the right time to think about what you'll do at a later point when you're really angered. Create an outline of your possible responses which will significantly improve your chances of not screaming at your child.

This way it is possible that when the time comes for us to respond and react, we will be able to give an easy and appropriate response without thinking too many.

Strategies to Teach with Positive Discipline

I'll share a few positive discipline methods that I really like and would like you to practice them frequently:

Let them make their own choices.

If you allow your toddler choices instead of instructions, you're less likely to find yourself in a normal situation of power battles. The choices empower your toddler.

Of course, ensure that you are happy with the choices you provide them. Don't offer your toddler an option you are unable to meet. If they do the child will start to doubt you.

Instead of saying "Hurry up dress in your shoes, you're running late," it is better to say "Do you prefer to put on your shoes first , or put on your jacket?" This will allow them to move much more smoothly.

The benefit of this positive discipline method is that you can encourage independence while still taking the reins of your aunt. Toddlers love autonomy, and will be thrilled to do it: we all have a chance to win!

It's not a good idea to ask a child to allow them to choose on everyday things but for him, each option is an opportunity to develop his independence.

It is because when we're toddlers the world seems to be centered around what "we have to do" through mandates and orders: "take medicine," "stop making noises," "go to bed right now."

If we could give you a choice of what to do, "that choice" is enough to lessen your resentment.

Environment Yes!

It is essential not to stifle this natural curiosity by continuously disciplining your child for touching items within the home.

As they grow older in age, their natural instinct is to be themselves and push boundaries. In this age it is vital to give the children the freedom they desire with respect to the boundaries.

For a toddler who is young it is crucial to make sure that the environment is "childproof" space. In other words, we should keep those potentially hazardous or delicate items away from reach (this helps reduce stress for parents as well as toddlers). Your child won't have to be told "no" every day and will feel more secure of peace of mind knowing that he's not putting his hands into things that which he shouldn't.

If you are using the word "no" in moderation, your child is more likely to listen when you speak it. So, whenever you can try to use positive language to end any challenging behaviour.

Help students understand emotions

It's never too late to begin teaching your toddler to express their feelings. Inability to comprehend the emotion or what it is that is typical cause for toddlers to behave badly.

For toddlers an easy table for emotions could be a good idea. You can also make a unique one by taking pictures of your child's emotions. It's a great task! If your child is older learn the words from this vocabulary of feelings list to increase their vocabulary of emotions so that they are able to express themselves correctly.

"Toddlers need to be aware of what they are feeling before asking adults to take control."

Do not ignore the bad behavior

It is important to pick your fights and select the ones you want to fight. The claim that you will not observe or hear about such actions is also acceptable. Although it's not one of the most optimistic strategies of the discipline to employ frequently, it can work very effectively for small issues.

If my child is playing with objects that aren't allowed to do (like mother's books) I'm able to ignore it at instances. If my child is secure and content and I'm not concerned about the object, then at the time it becomes necessary I'll take the object from the reach of my child.

Be aware that we're not policemen and are as exhausting as it can be. Everyone doesn't like being lectured. Therefore, let's get away from ourselves and our families. The child is about to be a baby and honestly do we really need breathing space? We can create and enjoy an environment that is more relaxing in our homes when we apply the right amount.

Sometimes, toddlers seek attention that is negative. We can take away the joy by ignoring the bad behaviour and the desire to duplicate these actions in the near future.

Play detective

Why is your child behaving in this way? Do you know specific days or times of the day when this behaviors are more likely to happen? Could other toddlers or other adults trigger the behavior? Are there any environmental conditions that could be contributing? (for instance, being too cold, too hot or too noisy, for example, too busy, or too excessive noise). Perhaps any of these conditions be a contributing factor? For example, allergy, illness, dietary changes, medications changing and hunger, party or large crowds or or changes in routine?

Another idea is to note down the times of the day the behavior is occurring. For older children it is possible to include them in the process of figuring out what is bothering them.

I have never regretted reviewing and asking myself what is causing this behaviour? This behavior serves an action. If you know the reason behind the behavior, you will know the best way to end it.

Be conscient

Keep your discipline in order. Your child should know what they should be doing and not. If they don't receive the same message repeatedly and don't know what to behave. This can be confusing and cause your child feel anxious.

Make sure you follow the same schedule each day. This means regular time for nap, meals and the time at which your child is free to play.

If you must move, notify your child ahead of time. This will force you to brace yourself and make it difficult for an entirely different routine.

A story that a child reads again could be a great help for any major transition for example, a move, a new brother or a death. Include a picture of the old house, the area and the new one in the event that you are moving. Write down exactly what's expected to take place. This will provide the child with an understanding of what's happening and will avoid a lot of problems with discipline.

Toddlers thrive in routine. If they are aware of what's happening, they're less likely to be impulsive. Also, you perform better when you know the reason your spouse had an awful day!

Fun and distraction

Fun is an excellent source for young children to make use of. Little ones have a short time to pay focus, and it can be utilized for your benefit. You can distract them from what is troubling them. Instead of giving up try something new to do or talk about growth, your child might be interested.

In "the period of the witches" when my child's behavior becomes a source of concern for me, I will move him to a different room or take him for an outing. A breath of fresh air appears to be helpful.

If your child is older it is possible to think more strategically regarding this. If you are constantly hearing complaints from your child that he is unfocused at school, enlisting him on an athletic team could aid in channeling his enthusiasm.

In the end, it comes down to that nobody is perfect However, we all can strive to improve. It's not a problem that we don't have the best solution for every scenario. But, by being aware of the increasing number techniques for positive discipline methods you can greatly increase our chance of reacting effectively.

Do you remember the way you were punished as an infant?

What does this mean for how you discipline your child?

What changes in the long term do you make to ensure application in positive discipline?

If you're currently using outdated methods of discipline, such as humiliation, whipping or shame that have proved ineffective Try to determine the source of the problem and figure out how it is possible to not fall to the same tactics at a later time. Admit to your child that you are sorry for these actions and begin applying positive discipline methods to begin noticing positive changes in the family relationship.

Methods for Discipline for Highly sensitive Children

It's not always difficult to manage children's discipline. However, it is particularly difficult for the parents of kids who have sensitive and emotional issues. Parents must learn ways to discipline their children in a way that is effective, particularly when they are extremely emotionally and sensitive.

The most satisfying jobs in the world is being a parent and everyone who is blessed to be parent is truly content. But, it's not always fast. Most of the time, hard work can be the best work.

Through this difficult work that we develop as individuals and parents, and occasionally have the opportunity to reward ourselves for those moments that help us stay in our path. If you are a highly emotionally or responsive child's parents the job can present additional problems.

What is the definition of highly sensitive children?

A child with a high degree of sensitivity is alert as well as quick in their reactions. They sense things more deeply. They are incredibly sensitive and aware of their surroundings and the way they move within the space.

If a child with a high degree of vulnerability is in distress, you need to convince them that it's normal to feel anxious and that they can re-do whatever they've tried in case they feel better. These words do not impact the child's feelings deeply.

Once we've mastered some of the characteristics and behaviors of a child that is extremely reactive How can parents help instruct and discipline their children? Here is a more thorough explanation of this.

How do you discipline highly sensitive children?

The first thing to note is that being extremely sensitive isn't an illness or a condition, but an attribute. Being sensitive is a great quality when children and parents know how to manage the deeper emotions and feelings.

Refuse to defend

As parents, our thoughts need to be acknowledged. As we remove kids from our lives, children can be (repeatedly) dissatisfied with our choices as human beings. They are also unhappy with their feelings, emotions and reactions. It's a good thing!

As parents, as parents, we must be aware of and validate our children's personal feelings. In thisregard, it is essential that we do not become being defensive, and that we do not feel becoming a victim to our emotions.

Chapter 8: Abc of Understanding Toddler Behavior

The behavior of toddlers can be difficult. The term "trouble two" isn't the "trouble two's for reasons of. As a parent, it's crucial to be aware that it's a normal aspect of the development of a child. At around 18 months old the child will want to have the entire world right at their feet. This is normal. It is typical that you as as a parent, would want to show your child that he or she is part of the family and needs to be part of the family.

From a managerial point of from a management point of child discipline and behavior management include:

Positive reinforcement for the behaviors you wish to see

Avoid behaviors that you don't want to be associated with.

Make use of time-outs for "out-of-control" behaviour

I frequently see parents are aware of the rules but aren't able to find a way to alter their child's behavior. Sometimes, you're too far away to notice what's happening.

By using an understanding of toddler behavior using the ABC of Learning, you will be able to comprehend the real issues for your child. Then you can apply the strategies described above successfully.

A stands for Antecedents. You need to think about "what occurs prior to an act of violence?" This is, for example, for understanding the causes of tantrums, what happens prior to the screaming.

B stands for Behavior. You have to know what kind of behaviour you're evaluating.

If your child is exhibiting some behaviors that you don't prefer, select one thing you'd like to change and begin by focusing on the behavior that you want to change.

C stands for Consequences - what happens when the behavior is initiated. What should you do? What's the best thing for your child? The answer is likely to be some form of attention.

You're now equipped with everything you require. You are aware of what triggers the behavior to the surface and what is the "reward" for the behavior is. To alter the behavior, you must not reward it the same way that you do. Try to avoid the behaviour.

What is Toddler Discipline?

The dictionary definition for "Discipline" is defined as "Training intended to develop the specific characteristics or patterns of behavior, including training that leads to mental or moral improvements."

In this light, let's look at how we can answer one of the top desires we all parents have. It is to raise a well-rounded child. However, if you seek parents' definition of "good" every person has their own definition and response for this. Some parents' respect and manners are important, but they are for other children, they must adhere to the family's rules, while others could emphasize characteristics like integrity, honesty, and kindness. In reality it's everything and more when given the right chance, your child can develop each one of them a part of his personality.

However, before we can move one we must answer an essential question:

What is the reason to discipline children?

to help them understand the notion of the difference between right and wrong. While toddlers and infants especially aren't capable of fully comprehending this concept, we can help them the impression that it is there through our actions and words.

To start seedlings of self-control. They won't sprout quickly, but if they are nurtured correctly they will eventually become the root of your child's behaviour.

To instill to teach respect for respect for the rights of others and emotions of others, in order to help your child can grow from an ego-centric toddler into a compassionate , loving adult.

to ensure that your child grows up to be an adult who is happy. A child who isn't disciplined is usually at risk for an unwelcome awakening and lots of unhappy in the world of.

As a caring parent What strategies can you employ to reach this goal of instilling good behaviour for your child? That is the question we are going to try to the answer to in the next section. We are sure that you can accomplish this by "Discipline". What exactly is discipline? Or what is the line between being disciplined and hard.

As a mom, I have to be constantly distracted by these issues and have trying to figure out how I can get there without interrupting my relationship with my child.

"Discipline is a sign of love to children. He requires guidance. If you love your child there is no notion of being harsh with the child. A parent should also not be scared to hang himself. If you've never been disliked from your kid, then you were never a parent."

Parents find discipline for toddlers to be a challenging area to manage because it is difficult to be too strict with children in the early years, particularly because they have a love and affection for their parents so much. If you've been to this post, you might be giving your child to indulge in too much and it is important to teach your child discipline if would like them to change their actions.

Many parents mistake the concept of discipline for toddlers as punishment, and that's not what you should be doing. Keep in mind that toddlers are young and are still learning how to conduct themselves and they shouldn't be expected to become a ideal child overnight. Your job as a parent, to educate and show your child how you would like to conduct themselves.

How can one accomplish this without resorting to smacking or screaming? One of the primary reasons why toddlers have screaming fits can be for attention. I can remember watching a video of a child screaming and screaming their head off, however when parents left the room the child stopped screaming, stood up and followed their parent around before screaming yet again!

The correct way to deal with this for children in such kinds of situations is to not bother the situation. If they don't get their own way , do not accept their demands, as they could treat you as a person who is a nuisance when they get older and be aware that they could be able to do much more. Be strong in these instances When they cease screaming to you, take them to a quiet place and tell them it isn't the kind of behavior you'd expect from them.

Keep up your word and be consistent when you make threats. Are you aware of times when you were in public and your child suddenly started acting up? If you have told them that they would not be able watch television this evening due to their behaviour, you must to stick with the treat or they'll discover the message you gave them is irrelevant and what they do will be unpunished.

Be aware to remember that the discipline for toddlers isn't just about punishment. It's essential to encourage the good behavior of your child. When they're happy and behave well that you're extremely pleased with them. Also, give them the best treatment. Maybe even take them out to somewhere. If you are able to encourage good behavior they will see that you are adamant about this and will lead to more respect.

It is crucial to Be a good disciplinarian for your toddler

Discipline doesn't only mean the punishments toddlers face. Instead, it makes sure that children acquire the knowledge they require to be responsible adults.

There are many kinds of discipline and different ways of parenting. In the end, no matter the kind of discipline that the parent employs discipline can provide toddlers with many advantages.

Discipline Helps Toddlers Manage Anxiety

It's true that toddlers aren't keen on being in the control of their parents. They will often test the limits to ensure that their caregivers are in a safe environment. When parents offer negative and positive consequences as toddlers develop, they learn and grow.

Toddlers with parents who are permissive often feel anxious because they are forced to make adult-like decisions. Lack of direction and lack of leadership can be extremely stressful for toddlers.

Discipline Teaches You How to make good choices

The proper use of discipline can teach toddlers to make the right decisions. For instance, if an infant loses the privileges of riding on his bicycle for cycling into the roadway and getting a ticket, he is taught how to make safer decisions the next time.

Healthy discipline can teach toddlers alternatives to getting their requirements satisfied. Toddlers must develop problem-solving abilities such as impulse control, as well as self-regulation from a disciplined and appropriate.

It is essential to differentiate the different between punishments and consequences. When toddlers are disciplined using appropriate consequences , they are taught from the mistakes they made. However, punishments can teach children to think that parents can be cruel or that they can "not be punished" whenever they do something wrong.

Discipline Teaches Toddlers how to manage Emotions

When a child gets an time-out for beating his sibling, he acquires techniques that can help him handle his anger better when he gets angry in the near future. The purpose of time-outs is to train your child how to put himself in time-out if they are upset, before he's in trouble.

Other strategies for discipline including praise can teach children how to manage their feelings. If you tell your child, "You are working so hard to make the tower, even though it's difficult. Keep up the great work," your child learns about the importance of accepting anger.

In the absence of a problem, it will teach toddlers appropriate social strategies to deal with their frustration and anger. If you don't accept an angry temper and your child learns that it's not the best method of getting his demands fulfilled. If you don't listen to the whining of your child, he will realize that whining doesn't alter your behaviour.

Discipline Keeps Toddlers Safe

The main purpose of discipline should be to ensure the safety of toddlers. This is a concern for safety concerns including checking both directions before crossing the street. There should be consequences if your child does not take proper safety security measures.

It is also important to address other health issues for example, the prevention of overweight. If you allow your child to indulge in whatever food she likes is likely to face severe health risks. It is important to establish healthy boundaries and provide information to help your child understand how to make healthier choices.

Define the motives for rules so that your child can understand the concerns. Instead of telling your child, "Stop jumping," the moment your child starts jumping onto the bed, inform the reason why it's not a good idea. Speak to him "You might fall and strike your head. This isn't a good idea."

If your child is taught the rationale for your rules and understands the particular dangers to his safety, he'll have a greater chance to take into consideration the risks to his safety even if you're not around to instruct him on what to do.

Chapter 9: Dealing with Tantrums
Ignoring Them vs. Rising Your Voice

There's always times that, despite your best intentions you have to raise your voice in order to draw your child's interest. In reality, if you only use it as a rarely employed tool, it could be very successful! However, as generally it can quickly diminish its effectiveness and cause tension within your relationship.

A toddler will suddenly be able for exploration of the environment within their. They'll swiftly progress from slow, shaky steps to running through the house or room. All they experience and come with can be both thrilling and frustrating. The nature of being too young usually implies that they are not able to manage their emotions completely and can result in a rage. In essence, their rage is simply a result of their frustration over having no ability to deal with the situation.

Raising Your Voice

A sudden, loud sound can bring peace in almost any circumstance regardless of whether it's an assembly room meeting or toddler's screaming. The instant result will end the screaming, but it's likely to be just for only a short time.

A toddler will immediately register your frustration and respond to it by intensifying the severity of their tantrum. This is even more likely in the event that you continue to rant and groan at them. Actually, the more you yell at your toddler the more likely that they'll switch off. Their attention span tends to be very short, so your shouting will have no impact on their temper.

It is true that shouting could lead to your toddler completing their temper tantrum. But, there are a variety of consequences of this that need to be taken into consideration:

Shouting creates Shouters

When you curse at your child They will think that it's acceptable to shout at people. It is common for them to shout at their home, at the playgroup or even at school. This can create an endless cycle that could be extremely difficult to break down in the future.

Fear and Respect

It is very likely that your child will be afraid of your anger outbursts. Although they might be effective in controlling them, they could harm your relationship in the long time. No good parent would want their child to be afraid of them!

Self-esteem

Research indicates that shouting at toddlers is a common occurrence throughout their life and, as a result, typically children who have low self-esteem. It is believed that shouting can reduce their ability to communicate with the other person or to reason. This can affect confidence in themselves, even though it's typically not apparent until they get older.

The yelling of your child is one of the subjects that receives an enormous amount of attention. Many parents and researchers agree that it provides little or no benefits. If everything was perfect parents would not shout. But, the mix of stressors you face throughout the day could result in a requirement to be shouting. It's not typically used to solve a problem but rather as a knee-jerk response when you're near the end of your rope.

Inattention to the Tantrum

Do you really want to be is to ignore your toddler? This method is more effective than you believe. The first step is to recognize that a toddler's temper tantrum happens because your child isn't able to manage their emotions. The use of temper tantrums is to reinforce the right behavior and assist your child to understand how to handle anger.

Many parents and scientists be of the opinion that the best approach to dealing with tantrums is to not pay attention to the issue. There are two explanations for this:

Stops the Tantrum

Children, particularly toddlers, will react to the way you respond. The more reassurance you provide the more likely they'll be to repeat the same behavior. If they discover that the rage they have expressed does not have any effect on the other person, they're more likely to stop their behavior and change their approach.

As toddlers is testing the boundariesof your child, and you react, making tantrums a normal way to grab your focus!

There's nothing else you can do

In most situations, there's nothing you can do to stop the rage once it's begun, and any kind of interaction could be perceived to your kid as an acknowledgment of their rage. Any attempt to rationalize with them will likely fail because you'll need to work through the initial tantrum, and in the end, your child might be unable to comprehend the strategies you're employing.

A temper tantrum is normal, however, following these steps will aid in ensuring that it is addressed quickly and not an ongoing issue:

Explain to your child that what they're doing will not earn them the reward they're looking for You can also inform them of the consequences of their rage will be.

Allow them to vent. If you're uncomfortable with them, walk away and observe them while ignoring them.

If your child is screaming at a public location, it's ideal to get your child picked up and take them to a private location. Your vehicle or a public restroom are the best choices.

If you have to speak to them about anything be sure to speak in a calm and calm voice. But, not mentioning them is the most effective approach.

It is important to not let your child when they show signs of aggression. In this situation it is essential to keep them in your arms to stop the risk of injury to them or other people.

In the end, if you can pinpoint what caused the tantrum then you can take your child from the situation. It is possible to distract the child by making funny faces or even a joke.

Once any outburst is over and you are satisfied, give your child a hug and a hug. This will calm them as well as remind them the rage was unneeded. Do not think about the incident!

Peacekeeping the Peace

It is essential to understand that there are instances that you just must maintain peace. One good way to do this is to be aware of the likelihood of a temper tantrum to occur and then defuse the situation before it turns into the reality. This will keep everyone satisfied!

There are many ways to minimize the possibility of a temper tantrum:

Planning

It's been proven that the majority of tantrums are caused by your child is exhausted or hungry. The majority of toddlers need an afternoon nap and it's important to ensure this. Also, you should plan your meal times or provide snacks to make sure they're happy and content while you cook food.

It is important to plan ahead so that your child doesn't feel thirsty or tired, This means they are less likely to be angry and throw the rage of a child.

Another great way to plan is to review the list of goals you would like to accomplish and then take a conscious decision not to complete everything if you are aware that your child is beginning to feel exhausted.

Connecting

A strong bond with your kid can assist in ensuring they are able to behave properly and will also help to prevent children from having a temper tantrum. This is especially important in the case of being working all day. Your child will be thrilled to meet you, but disappointed when you aren't spending time with them. This could cause them to be angry and throw a tantrum.

Therefore, it is essential to spend time with your child because it will stop the anger from forming early on.

Bartering

A key way to avoid tantrums is to discuss the issue with your child. They're trying to make their stamp on the world and often, tantrums occur due to the fact that they don't have what they need. If your child desires something, accept the desire. Then, you can let them have their desire... as long as they first complete something else.

For instance If they would like the same toy that their sibling already has, create an activity to win the item. This can help them share and keep them from becoming upset.

It is crucial to keep your sentences short while doing this because it will make sure your child understands what you are saying.

Check the Anger

You might be able to do this prior to the tantrum begins. If that isn't the scenario, then be patient for a couple of hours after the event has concluded by asking your child why they seem to become angry. If they are able to focus and communicate their thoughts then their anger will diminish. They'll also be able face a variety of emotions and emotions. This is something that a lot of people have trouble with!

Make sure they are safe

If you've been able to settle the issue prior to the tantrum, there's the chance that your child will be crying. Do not be concerned about the tears. If they are willing to hold them, you are free to do so. If not, remain close to them, since this will calm them.

Chapter 10: Strategies To Prevent Toddler Tantrums During Flights

The journey of a toddler with an allegation is not a problem, as well during a flight. The capable ancestor is equipped with the right accoutrements and methods to avoid the annoyances of toddlers in airports as well as biking terrors.I'm sure you've heard of the contempo beatings of the past that were told to get off the aircraft after having their three-year-old was again scolded from her bench to ensure alertness for the takeoff. For many parents, this variety of issues could be their suffering from a bike accident. Of course, children, as adults, tend to enjoy their good days, as well as their less-than-perfect days. Even the most airy and tolerant child, they can have an unforgiving return to frightened sick, scared, or exhausted.Foregoing the possibility of a complete catastrophe What kinds of actions can parents do to make toddler biking as smooth and easy as is possible? What can be done to ensure that toddler tantrums at the airport be prevented. Maintain the same routine. One of the best ways to prevent toddler-bike accidents is to adhere to your child's schedule as much as you can. The established adds security, stability and a lot of fun for your child's activities in the midst of a changing and potentially frightening environment. Be sure to give candy at the appropriate time. Make room for nap times. If you're able to you can, inform your bike or abettor to schedule an air trip at an hour when your child will usually be sleeping. Accede aerial at off-peak times. If you travel backwards at night, it may not just put your adolescent to go to sleep however, the airport could be less crowded, less noise, and much easy to navigate. 2. Nix the questionable training. If your child is not from Absurd Training 101, now is not the ideal moment for an additional lesson. In diapers (or disposable pull-ups) for a scattering of hours can provide plenty of tension for your child and less stress for the child as opposed to the disgusting and odorless worst-case scenario. 3. Toys to accompany. As well as additional toys. Pack many of your favorite books (and possibly a book on airplanes) as well as baby toys that aren't noisy as well as a few items of abundance (such as a beloved blanket). Do you have a portable DVD player? If not, you can borrow one from a family member. Take along a pair of movies suitable for your child. It is also possible to take a difficult toy out for the right reward. 4. Haversack benefits. If your child is enough to scratch a baby's backpack, let them place their favorite objects inside to it. The process of cutting it open, unzipping it and taking objects from it, could be a ball that you can play with and then action in the direction you think you are claiming it the most. 5. Pick seats with windows. The view from the window can be an incredibly relaxing diverting. The view above the plane window also provides educational possibilities and possibilities.6. Fly continuously. Make sure to do this if possible. This eliminates the conflict between adjoining flights.7. Set boundaries. Before departure, communicate your toddler what must be acceptable to them during the trip. Let your child accept (to the greatest extent of your child's understanding) it is expected that you be a mixture of the sitting and the arena quietly.8. Booty cost. Be aware that you are the adult. It is your personal responsibility to take care of issues before they become a problem. Since you know the best option for your child and your family, you will be able to handle your adolescent in a tender but respectful manner.Make every achievement a reason to love your time travelling with your child. Don't allow a casual acknowledgment from an angry adolescent driver ruin your journey. Be as friendly as you can to the people around you, but keep in mind that your safety, health and well-being of your adolescent's top priority.

Chapter 11: Toddler Discipline Techniques - Language Strategies For Stressed Parents

Most of the time Restraining toddlers can be a raising anxiety for guardians. It can be difficult managing toddlers who are screaming at, kicks, screaming and throwing every one of those temper flares. Parents must employ methods of discipline for toddlers to be competent for raising respectful toddlers and enjoy parenting a child.

One crucial aspect that parents should be aware of is the importance of using compelling correspondence. Utilizing methods of communication, parents can impart discipline-focused messages on their children.

Guardians should be aware of the importance of using positive words when communicating with their children. Avoid using words that are marked, for example, terrible devious, sly and other negative portrayals. Children can be influenced emotionally, causing low confidence. Instead of telling them to "stop" or "no," guardians must define what exactly they want their toddlers to accomplish. They should not use the words "Stop" or "no" are not enough if they are they are used as frequently as is possible. Use these words only for important occasions, not for every day conversations with your children. Toddlers, just like grown-ups are likely to listen to us if we guiding them in a direction that is not something we're not requiring to tell them.

If you are addressing your toddlers specifically in their screaming attacks, parents must remain still and not shout. No matter if guardians use positive or negative language and phrases, the manner in which they express their thoughts may affect or diminish the effectiveness of your toddler's actions to control their behavior. If you shout more frequently than not, you're altering your toddler's view that this is normal, and that he is likely to not hear you further.

Guardians can use certain language patterns that can be utilized to talk with toddlers on a daily basis dependent on the context. These language patterns can be used as toddler discipline methods include the use of neuro-phonetic programming , also known as NLP. Through the joining of NLP concepts, parents are able to without much effort convince their children to do their job.

Step-by-step directions for handling toddler discipline

The one thing that most guardians don't want to enforce is disciplining their children, particularly in the case of an infant. I hate toddler discipline, but it's difficult to keep a distance from it when your child is heavily distracted. What can gain direct benefit from being off base?

As a child I received an occasional good hit occasionally, however now I realize that I was worthy of it. However, in current society, parents look at various types of toddler discipline, and refrain from using physical force.

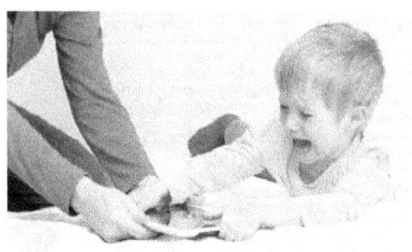

Even as a toddler during the beginning stages of life, it is important to establish a few basic guidelines. There aren't many, but around 4 , or 5, is an acceptable number. The first thing to consider is

Remember when you set these guidelines is that you must remain consistent with the principles. If you establish guidelines, then at this point you must adhere to the rules generally. There's no need to. Inform your child about what your rules are and the next time they do something wrong, let them know. one of them, they must do it again, each time they violate it. Your child should also be aware that as the parent, they must follow the rules you set out for them.

Toddlers can be polite, but often as they are terribly behaved. If they're polite, then you can show your child appreciation, and this will reassure them that with good conduct they will be praised, but when they engage in offensive behavior, they be punished.

When your child is out of the way, then you should demonstrate with a firm , clear voice. If they're asked to destroy the television for instance, but they don't make a fuss, say "Do what I say," don't say it with a rage. If your toddler's behavior isn't working, and your child is not being respectful, don't allow them to. If you allow this, it is a clear signal to them that they'll be insubordinate the next time around and follow your instructions.

A powerful form that toddlers can be disciplined is to break. If your child is refusing to cooperate to the break, you may transfer them to a breakroom or even a space. Make sure your child is aware that they must remain in the area so that they can think about their behavior. Inform your toddler that you will keep them on the break-room or break-room until they are ready to sit down and talk to you about their conduct. This is an essential method of discipline that is well-known because it works.

Effective Toddler Discipline Using Positive Language Communication

The first-time caregivers will most likely encounter difficulties in managing their children. If they're not educated about how to handle their children effectively It can be uncomfortable. Toddlers may begin to exhibit dangerous behaviors when they reach the age of two. They're not called "awful 2s" in their own way. The habits associated with hissy fits are likely to be felt until the seventh year. It is vital for parents to be provided right from the beginning with the appropriate methods for their children to be able to head-begin for restraining their infants.

One important aspect that parents should be aware of when it comes to child discipline concerns the optimal usage of language with their children. The choice of words could affect the way children are treated. It is crucial to use positive words more often when speaking to your children, especially when you're preparing your own discipline talks.

Studies have shown that you'll get more success in having your message understood by children, and even adults using positive language instead of negative ones. Do you notice how a simple "Don't do this" isn't necessarily effective in stopping your children from doing an unjust act? It is possible that you will be more active in guiding me. Just like adults, toddlers almost surely tune out if we instruct them, rather than explaining to them what to do.

Parents must also stop from portraying their child's behaviour as a snarky, unpleasant as well as other unfavorable words. Children can be affected by their environment and this can make them behave more in a negative manner. It could also lead to lower confidence.

Five Steps for Better Toddler Behavior - 5 Steps for a Better Toddler Conduct

The discipline of a toddler is one that stands out among the most essential requirements for the development of a respectable child, however for some parents this could seem like a burden. This is why we have listed five aspects of the disciplinesystem that have been proven to be extremely effective in establishing an enduring relationship and enhancing the sense of security between toddler and their parents.

Break

This is among the most well-known methods of reinforcing a toddler. The child "offender" is taken into a corner, or "insidious place" for a period. It's crucial that this duration isn't too long, allow one minute for each age group. It is possible to stay in the vicinity of them, but ideally by your side or back towards them, so that they won't be able to draw attention to your back.

When time has passed by, gently remind your child using everyday language the incident and remind them that if they repeat it or repeat it, they'll have to face some other break.

It is essential that discipline takes place in the time of incident, therefore you need to be prepared to enforce your children even when they are away from home. Make it a habit to do so in the gaze of other people to ensure that the child's confidence doesn't suffer.

Diversion and Diversification

The most popular methods to discipline your toddler is to redirect them. It is a quick way to distract the child from what they're planning to do and direct the attention of your child to something "more safe" and gradually positively, for example, helping your family around the house. In this way they'll be living the good life, rather than continuing to follow the path, causing inexplicably "inconvenience."

Unmindful of Temper Tantrums

Hissy fits are a way to display extreme emotions. It is essential that your toddler quickly realizes that their tics aren't able to deal with the situation or even you. There are two methods to accomplish the task (a) by ignoring the behavior completely and (b) by saying that you would like to witness their dishonest actions and telling them that after they've completed their act the task, you'll talk to the child about it.

Through training, you'll probably be able to quickly defuse the situation and discuss it with them in a calm and peaceful manner.

Feedback that is positive

It's been observed that encouraging feedback is a popular choice for toddlers than discipline. Instead of always telling them "no" when they do something wrong when they mess up, look for the things that they excel at and give them lots of constructive criticism as well as affection. Try not to become the usual scolder.

Establishing Limits and Rules

Toddlers are typically adventurous and curious, which is why they require standards and boundaries established for them to ensure they are safe and free of any disturbance. They feel safer and loved by those who help them to understand the reason for these rules were set. It is essential that the guidelines you create are simple and easy for children to grasp it. Also, they should be linked in a reliable manner, so your child is not confused.

Five different methods for encouraging and establishing toddler discipline have proven effective for certain guardians and should most likely perform for you. This is just the beginning. Toddlers develop quickly, and there's much more you can do to find out to help make those "growing up" times a joyful and rewarding time for both the child and parent. There's a wealth of fantastic advice on the internet.

Toddler Discipline: A Big Problem Awaits

One of the most difficult things in life is becoming the parent of your child. Parenting is a skill you develop along the way. It's often a bumpy road of high as well as low ones. Certain people may find raising children less difficult than others, however the ideal parent doesn't just mean to show your child love, but also to teach them the distinctions between good and bad. It is usually done as child discipline. If your child is a mess and is unable to control them, restraining them shows them they've messed up. If they are doing well, we show them that what they've accomplished is good and reward for their actions in a certain way.

When you take any test, and especially raising children, you'll be able to enjoy your good times and bad ones. The pace of things can be rapid after a certain point, and after which they will turn completely upside down the next.

One thing that guardians have to struggle with is child discipline. It is a problem for any parent that is not only parents with no experience. One kind of discipline for toddlers could be effective on one child, but it's not effective for another.

This is the test you must pass by determining which types of discipline work for your child and what will not work. It's all about experimenting.

Every toddler needs discipline. Without discipline, how can they to understand what is proper and what's not? They are also taught that they're in charge of their own actions. It teaches them what constitutes good behavior and what constitutes bad practice.

The most important thing to be aware of when using your chosen kind to discipline your child is regardless the toddler's reaction with it. You must be quiet. This will help you remain in control and makes it clear your role as the one in charge regardless of any freak outs or temper tantrums that your toddler could throw up, you are the one who is in control.

Whatever happens, regardless of whether you end in restraining your child or not, you must always give them love and affection regardless of how stressed within you they might make you feel. Your child must realize you care about them. If you share a strong connection, at this time, chances are that the more obedient your child will be and this is what everyone wants.

Toddler Discipline

The toddler's behavior is always according to all accounts worse when you're away with your toddler. Rage, crying and issues with behavior can be risky and every once in some time, they will think about going anywhere. The behavior issues can occur in the office of a specialist, in the restaurant, at the recreational centers... anywhere you're tempted to go. When you take everything into consideration how can you get rid of or at the very least, redirect the rage, crying, and other behavior problems? Toddlers aren't going to stop being toddlers. They are exploring and learning. They are demanding and stubborn. It could be as simple as having a few items to help keep your child engaged and fully engaged. When your toddler is in a rush can be controlled by using:

A Activities Bag... The pack should contain an additional toy, a pastels and shading books as well as a storybook, basic activities and games that toddlers can engage in.

Portable DVD player... This DVD player portable can entertain a toddler for up to 15-30 minutes.

Toddler DVDs... DVDs that are easy to use and motion-pictures for young children.

These suggestions do involve you carrying and moving things or sacks everywhere you travel. Whatever the case the suggestions will assist in reducing the frequency of crying, rage or other issues with behavior. Utilizing these tools will assist in making your journey enjoyable for your child. You'll be able to collaborate with your child to show them how to conduct their manner of conduct in the open and allow everyone else to enjoy a memorable trip too.

Now you're able to go everywhere with your toddler, and being able to keep your child entertained, engaged and happy even in a rush!

How to deal with toddlers - Parenting Tips for Dealing With Your Toddlers

Being a parent to toddlers isn't so simple because rage-related episodes during toddlerhood are among the most difficult issues for parents, for what it's worth during this stage, your toddler may make you question your knowledge. Your toddlers might have their own set of standards and they may not be able to listen or suddenly possess their own way of communicating everything that has to be conveyed through shouting, in this case the ability to control these issues at this age is vital.

Between the ages of one and three, children are enthralled at a myriad of things and they like to explore and record. It is possible to see them getting into drawers, opening everything, mixing the fishbowl with the pets, or looking at the contents of your bag and even observing your child kissing her lips with your lipstick if she's watched your lips being covered.

In this age of children who are fascinated by things and throw a few fits often, here are a couple of tips to aid you manage children and their behavior.

Create a safe place for your baby. It isn't impossible to stop the baby from investigating things, climbing furniture , and exploring the surroundings since these are part of his development. It's not ideal to let your child in the dark while they perform their work. It is possible to control this something that may harm his back, repair broken furniture and spread electrical attachments keep clearing things out of his reach and maintain your eye on the child.

Don't be apathetic to their outbursts of anger. When it comes to managing toddlers, it is important to realize that they will, for the majority of the time will listen to you when they get angry and you need to be extremely patient. Don't be a slave to his demands constantly. Most toddlers who get into their tempers are seeking for attention and one way to handle it is to not pay attention until the child calms down. Then, he will put down.

Get him distracted, let him go, or give him your options depending on the situation. If he isn't keen on receiving the item he wants it is possible to offer alternatives in addition. In all likelihood, it is possible to be difficult even for children to obtain the things they need. Give them a toy that they can choose from or other vegetables if the child doesn't require the primary one. If you're open clearly, you shouldn't leave him alone. You have to finish the situation if he's not quieting down.

Define which topics are debatable and which are not debatable in terms of controlling toddlers and their bouts of outrage. If your child is begging to wear a pink dress instead of the one you're wearing then do not be concerned about it. But, when it comes to ever-growing issues that affect his security as well as his health, the like, you must not be lenient and adhere to the rules.

Find out the distinct factors that trigger his episodes of outrage. In most cases, they'll have a rage attack in the event of being tired or hungry and therefore, you'll be required to deal with the root of the issue first. Make sure that you're providing your child with the right nutrition because this can also cause emotional issues for your young child.

Toddlers and their bouts of outrage can be a test of your understanding , however since they're all an element of their development and are not a choice however, there are avenues that make this time easier for you and your child.

Chapter 12: The Absorbent Mind and Conscious Mind

What is an absorbent mind?

In accordance with according to the American Montessori Society, the insatiable thoughts begin from until about the age six. The infant is engaged in a period of overly intellectual activities that allows children to" absorb" the knowledge of the world around them without conscious effort, easily and naturally. Toddler does not only absorb his language but rather the habits of his family and the community. He learns how to behave under positive circumstances He also learns about what foods to eat. While some of it is explicitly taught, a lot of it is focused on the capabilities of the toddler's mind. The child's mind could be compared to an dig cam that snaps photos of all that it observes through the lens, or to a sponge taking in the entire world around it. The information that a child absorbs at some point over the duration of the thought becomes a result and forms the foundation of their character. The thoughts of the absorbent can be divided into two categories that include the unconscious level and the conscious level.

The Unconscious Stage 3 to 0 Years Old

At this point the child absorbs information without conscious thought or awareness. They learn to stand, sit, walk and talk without making an conscious effort. Little ones will watch all of it with no any discrimination or desire. The baby for all of the time period is likely to mimic what they observe. The subconscious power does not anymore have any goals or objectives for example, a baby who has a skewed view of the back is building his muscles and spine however , he's not aware of this fact. He is completely in line with the natural laws. In this stage the child also learns from his surroundings the language. He begins to think about the language. He is absorbed by the traditions that surround him. They then become to become part of his.

The Conscious Phase During The Ages of 3 to 3-6 Years Old

When we reach the age of 3 at which point we start to notice the beginnings of awareness which indicates the start of recall and conscious focus. The toddler still is a sponge which absorbs information quickly but she's now actively search for positive results from her studies. A toddler at this age is expanding her newly acquired schools and abilities. They are predisposed to learning things such as order, sequencing and tunes, numbers and letters, which eventually result in analysis, math, and writing skills. The child is beginning to show an intense desire to be completely independent with no assistance. She hopes to be the ultimate master of her thoughts as well as her frame and surroundings. Anyone who provides unnecessary assistance or encourages dependence can become a hindrance towards the kid. The ability of Montessori to harness the power of their thoughts in the beginning of their existence is a remarkable benefit. As parents and educators we must recognize that the child's mind is unique that we have and learn methods to aid the child use this incredible absorbent thought process to their advantage.

The Functions of The Absorbent Mind

Through the power of mind, the child achieves two significant creative works. In actuality, he creates or constructs all the elements of his character and intelligence and is able to adapt to the society within which he lives. The consciousness that is consuming of the infant absorbs all experience of the world, and then becomes an integral part, and forming it. It doesn't happen through inheritance or intuitive thinking, or just growth, but is the result of the capacity for creativity in the infant. The infant is the one who does the work. Montessori writes "The kid isn't an impassive entity who owes everything we can give him in the sense that he's been a empty vessel is ours to fill. It is actually the child who creates the person. No person is more made through the child that he was."The absorption of the mind is one of the most crucial concepts in the early childhood education.. The thoughts that absorb enable us to live our adult lives. The brain is an absorbent capacity of a sponge to absorb which is essential in creating an individual from their specific subculture. It's pleasant to think about children's thoughts until the age of around six, and there will be a shift to the thinking processes we have as adults.

Every toddler is taught to speak in his mother language. No one is able to teach him vocabulary grammar, syntax, or syntax. Every day, this happens in all countries at all the time. It's a truly amazing achievement! If you've attempted to master a foreign language in the future you'll realize it's not as easy. Every toddler experiences its part to make. What does it happen? Through their absorbing minds. If the child is in an the environment in which she can hear the spoken language, she will speak it. As she absorbs the words and their meanings along with the context and emotional meaning behind them the kid begins to develop the capacity to communicate. Children learn not just their language , but also the nuances of their family and friends. They are taught about the foods we eat, as well as how to behave in certain circumstances. A portion of this is explicitly taught, but a huge majority of it is learned through the child's brain. Children absorb through an educational system called "mental chemical chemistry" and develop their identities and themselves through what they learn.

To explore the thoughts of the mind along with the rational thoughts Let's compare a picture with a sketch.

In the photo, each aspect is precisely in the exact way it was intended such as the color, feeling, the attitude as well as the past. It's a lot more fixed and persists because it changed over time as the photo was taken. In the drawing, the amount of detail can be as high or as small as the artist decides. It could be the idea of the artist's cup instead of any specific cup, and it could be made up of background. The thoughts that absorb are more similar to the dig camera. The information that the child takes in through the contemplation process can be easily translated into outcomes and remains as the basis of their character. What is taken in by the child later on in the thought process is processed through aware working and memory, but may not be as essential to the persona. From the time of birth until at least the age of 6, the child has a powerful and attentive mind. The baby is very young and cannot decide which things to concentrate his focus on or what to play music as an adult's alert and rational mind is able to do. In contrast the mind acts like a camera exploring the entire world of his surroundings.

Montessori's knowledge of the power of the mind that is absorbed in the early years of life is a wonderful gift. It shows us how we can provide a healthy environment for the child's first year and, as he truly is in the environment the environment, he is absorbed and grows. In the Montessori early child program for between the ages of 2 1/2 and 6 years old, we expose the youngsters to many thrilling activities, in addition to math, language, science of music, the sciences and geometry. With the help of the absorbing mind we are able to give our children with a broad and solid foundation. Moreover, it is extremely convenient for students to conduct research. With the amazing "mental chemical" of the mind that is absorbed that the child creates his or her own identity through many passions. The child develops through a the choice of a self-selected, appealing hobby, and develops a solid foundation of a focused and thoughtful approach to on a solid foundation of.

A visit to the Symphony for father and boy, for example, yields extremely positive reviews for every single one of them. Adults are able to focus on a specific area of interest and avoid distractions. The child hasn't yet developed this capability and may have a difficult to keep his attention on the music. You can expect him to remember lots of details about the experience that the structure changed into , what the people the people who moved into it and what they carried and so on. The child takes in these memories without any effort on his part. Though he is able to absorb an incredible variety of impressions however, he's not always capable of accessing these memories because he hasn't been able to classify the information he's receiving. Memories are stored in the storehouse of toddler impressions, but they're all mixed together and don't have any value, but they are beneficial for the child.

The Sensorial curriculum is developed to aid the child's ability to revisit those initial impressions that may be stored, and to refine and crystallize his understanding of the ideas. The materials themselves attract the typical tendencies for working and precision and assist the child to achieve those objectives. Through his involvement with Sensorial substances, he'll discover how to categorize his experiences and, as his attention increases, he'll begin building his brain. "Our sensory material provides an idea of a guideline to make a comment for it categorizes impressions that all senses can get: the sounds, colors, notes as well as sizes and forms as well as odors, touch-sensations and taste. This is also a kind of subculture for it causes us to take notice of ourselves as well as to the world around us. In addition to writing and speech it is among the kinds of culture that enhances the persona and boosts its natural powers.

A child between the ages of three and six is also a motor-sensorial learner. The brain is constantly collecting impressions, but it's now extremely inspired with the help of his enthralling enjoyment of the environment. His hands are believed to be the tools of his brain and the need to work and study is extremely efficient. Dr. Montessori spoke extensively about the common tendencies of males and how orientation and exploration are among the most effective motivations for young children. She created the environment in the study area to encourage exploration and discovery. Through the child's exploration and discovery, he becomes more aware of his surroundings and is able to explore it more independently. A major and crucial instruction that manuals provide at the beginning of a toddler's time in the classroom is listening games that are designed to aid in orienting himself to his environment and expand his memory of auditory. "The young child's initial movements were instinctual. Now, he is acting consciously and in a voluntary manner and this leads to the awakening of his soul. The ability to be aware of will is one that grows with time and play. The goal of improving the need to improve it. is a slow process that is cultivated through continuous activities with the world around us.

We must make use of the ability of children to absorb elements of their environment as well as the desire to be involved in research into the world surrounding him. We've observed for us how children from the age of three to six have an incredibly easy ability to learn new vocabulary. In the children's residence software, we use this ability for language by offering materials that help our kids start to study more about the world surrounding them. We start by teaching children how to differentiate between living and non-living. We then teach him how to classify living things into animal life or plant life. In the next step, he'll be taught about the five classes of vertebrates, namely chicken, Reptile, Amphibian, Mammal and Fish. If a child shows a particular interest in learning about sharks, turtles or ocean animals, then we will include these in our Language shelf. The activities are presented orally in dialogues that are initiated by the book. By adding a label on the identical Language photo playing cards we can also draw children of a certain age splendor, and they are becoming proficient readers.

Conscious Mind

The information we gather through our senses as we grow is stored as well as stored within our subconscious thoughts. Alongside this sensory information as well as the expectations and ideals we construct out of it are recorded too. When we leave our childhood behind many of this content will be a part of us and influences on our actions. Researchers have discovered a top-quality kind of brain wave which we can detect primarily upon their frequencies. From the very lower phases of interest recorded by the deep sleep delta wave, to more powerful frequencies that are recorded in beta waves in the conscious mind. As children grow their brains, the primary frequencies of their brains shift from slow to faster waves. This means they are moving from the unconscious mind to the conscious mind.

Delta Waves and The Unconscious Thoughts

Since to the instant of our first breath until about 2 years old our brains work predominantly with waves of low frequency. When you are asleep adults sleep at the lower end of the range. This is the reason why infants typically cannot remain awake for very long. Therefore, the reason for this is mostly in the subconscious. They are able to filter and correcting the data they receive from the external world. In this day and stage, the pleasures associated with"the "wondering mind" the neocortex could be extremely diminutive.

Zeta Waves

After a period of between 2 and five or six years old the children start to show only marginally improve their EEG numbers. Children who "stay in the zeta" remain in a state of consciousness like the trance state. They also are more connected to their own internal world as opposed to the outside world. They live in the realm of imagination and abstract thought. Their basic and rational thinking isn't very developed. This is why young children are more likely to believe in the whole thing they are taught to believe that there is Santa Claus, for example. As they get older such things could have a profound effect on girls: attractive girls are calm. Boys do now not cry. Your brother is more intelligent than you are. Try this. You'll fail. You're a poor child... the forms of words are immediately transferred into their subconscious, since brain waves that are slower control the subconscious.

Everything the toddler is exposed to and hears will be arranged into the form of concepts. These ideals determines their behavior and the way they perceive reality at some point during adulthood. This is why it's essential to train your children in this way. Once you have figured out this fact, you must be accountable for it.

Alpha Waves

From the age of five to eight years old their brain waves change with a slightly higher frequency. The analytical mind starts to form, which allows children to draw conclusions and draw conclusions about the rules of law that govern their external living. However their own inner world of imagination can be exactly the same way as the outside world. Children of this age typically have one foot on each world. This is why they love playing with their feet. In this case, for instance, you ask a child to imagine he's in the ocean as a dolphin or for snowflakes blown up by the wind or as a superhero who is trying to save a person they can play the role for many hours.

Beta Waves

Between the ages of 8-12 years old and beyond brain-related activities increase at greater frequency. These types of waves continue until the age of maturity and increase in various levels. At the age of 12 years old, the doors between the conscious and unconscious mind usually closes. Beta waves are classified into three waves that are medium, small and high. As children enter the age of childhood they move from low-range beta waves high-variety and mid-variety wave, similar to the ones we observe in the majority of adults. After you've gotten a general understanding of how brain waves function and how they function, keep in mind that the data that your subconscious mind absorbs during your first seven years of existence still has a bearing on your present life. But, once you've learned to understand your own mind, you'll be able to control and alter the form that the impact on your life takes. If you have children in your supervision... Be careful about what you say to them due to the trust they place in you. Be gentle with them and tell that they are valuable to you and how wonderful they are. Encourage them to be awestruck by every single one of them. This will be the most important thing they do for throughout their lives.

Chapter 13: Brain Development In The Early Years

When we speak of developing the brain, we refer to the entire growth of your toddler. This includes the physical, the social and emotional realm. In the past few years, some breakthroughs have been made of what actually happens in the brain of a child and how their brains develop.

There are a few actions you can take as a parent to aid your child's development. As soon as your baby is born the first million connections are formed in their brains. These connections are the ones responsible for making the foundation for their development and learning. Every interaction you have with your child daily can influence the way these connections are made. It doesn't take a lot of time or money to aid your child's development.

The initial five years are vital. But that doesn't mean that you need to do it every time. The focus is on taking advantage of the early years and utilizing these as a great opportunity to get your child on the right track to get them off to a good start.

The Factors that Influence the brain development of your child

Research on brain development has revealed the existence of three primary elements that affect your child's brain development as well as their overall growth. They are:

Genes,

Experiments and

Relationships

Genes

Our lives are shaped by an genetic blueprint. We all get our traits and behaviours from our parents. What happens when children become adults is that two extremely important elements begin to emerge. The first is our daily experience and the second, relationships.

Experiments

Children go through everyday experiences that establish the foundations on the which their development and growth are constructed. Brains are constructed from the bottom upwards and development takes place through the brain. Therefore everything you do for children from the very beginning creates the basis for their future growth.

Relationships

Kids thrive when they have solid and loving relationships that are the most influential on the development of their brains. Each time you show love and take care for or do something for the children in your life, you establish the bond that supports the development of your child.

Simple things you can do to Support Your Child's Development.

If you inquire about what parents want for their children the following is the answer they will all give "we want our children to be healthy, happy and lead a happy life." It is possible.

Conclusion

I hope this book is useful in helping you manage your toddler's behavior in a healthy and positive manner.

Next, you must stay in line with positive discipline and reinforce your child's behavior by giving praise and rewards occasionally.

Thank you for your kind words and best wishes!

www.ingramcontent.com/pod-product-compliance
Lightning Source LLC
Chambersburg PA
CBHW071839080526
44589CB00012B/1054